D1207359

EXTINCT SPECIES

EXTINCT INVERTEBRATES AND PLANTS

First published in 2002 by
Grolier Educational
Sherman Turnpike
Danbury, Connecticut 06816
© Quartz Editions 2002

All rights in this book are reserved. No part of this book may be used or reproduced in any manner whatsoever or transmitted in any form or by any means, electronic or mechanical, including photocopying, recording, or any information storage and retrieval system, without written permission of the copyright owner except in the case of brief quotations embodied in critical articles and reviews. For information, address the publishers:

Grolier Educational, Sherman Turnpike, Danbury, Connecticut 06816.

Library of Congress Cataloging-in-Publication Data

Extinct species.

p. cm.

Contents: v. 1. Why extinction occurs - - v. 2. Prehistoric animal life - - v. 3. Fossil hunting - - v. 4. Extinct mammals - - v. 5. Extinct birds - - v. 6 Extinct underwater life - - v. 7. Extinct reptiles and amphibians - - v. 8. Extinct invertebrates and plants - - v. 9. Hominids - - v. 10. Atlas of extinction.

Summary: Examines extinct species, including prehistoric man, and discusses why extinction happens, as well as how information is gathered on species that existed before humans evolved.

ISBN 0-7172-5564-6 (set) - - ISBN 0-7172-5565-4 (v. 1) - - ISBN 0-7172-5566-2 (v. 2) - - ISBN 0-7172-5567-0 (v. 3) - - ISBN 0-7172-5568-9 (v. 4) - - ISBN 0-7172-5569-7 (v. 5) - - ISBN 0-7172-5570-0 (v. 6) - - ISBN 0-7172-5571-9 (v. 7) - - ISBN 0-7172-5572-7 (v. 8) - - ISBN 0-7172-5573-5 (v. 9) - - ISBN 0-7172-5574-3 (v. 10)

1. Extinction (Biology) - - Juvenile literature. 2. Extinct animals - - Juvenile literature. [1. Extinction (Biology) 2. Extinct animals.] I. Grolier Educational.

QH78 .E88 2002

578.68 - - dc21

2001055702

Produced by Quartz Editions
Premier House
112 Station Road
Edgware HA8 7BJ
UK

EDITORIAL DIRECTOR: Tamara Green
CREATIVE DIRECTOR: Marilyn Franks
PRINCIPAL ILLUSTRATOR: Neil Lloyd
CONTRIBUTING ILLUSTRATORS: Tony Gibbons, Helen Jones
EDITORIAL CONTRIBUTOR: Graham Coleman

Reprographics by Mullis Morgan, London
Printed in Belgium by Proost

ACKNOWLEDGMENTS

The publishers wish to thank the following for supplying photographic images for this volume.

Front & back cover t SPL/J.Baum & D.Angus

Page 1t SPL/J.Baum & D.Angus; p3t SPL/J.Baum & D.Angus; p7tr Glasgow Museum; p8br NHPA/S.Krasemann; p9tl NHPA/D.Woodfall; p9b NHPA/M.Tweedie; p10l NHPA/D.Heuclin; p11tl NHM; p11br NHPA/T.Kitchin & V.Hurst; p12tr Glasgow Museum; p12b Glasgow Museum; p13t Glasgow Museum; p13cl Glasgow Museum; p13br Glasgow Museum; p18tl NHPA/B.Hawkes; p19t OSF/H.Taylor; p19br NHPA/K.Schafer; p21t NHPA/J.Shaw; p21bl NHPA/G.Edwardes; p21br OSF/P.McCullagh; p22tl NHPA/S.Krasemann; p22bl NHPA/S.Krasemann; p24bc NHM; p26tr NHM; p26bl NHPA/G.Bernard; p33t NHPA/G.Bernard; p35tc NHPA/S.Dalton; p35br MEPL; p43t OSF/M.Black; p43br NHPA/E.Janes; p44tl RBG; p45tl RBG; p45br RBG

Abbreviations: Mary Evans Picture Library (MEPL); Natural History Museum (NHM); Natural History Photographic Agency (NHPA); Oxford Scientific Films (OSF); Royal Botanic Gardens (RBG); Science Photo Library (SPL); bottom (b); center (c); left (l); right (r); top (t).

EXTINCT SPECIES

EXTINCT INVERTEBRATES AND PLANTS

GROLIER EDUCATIONAL

SHERMAN TURNPIKE, DANBURY, CONNECTICUT 06816

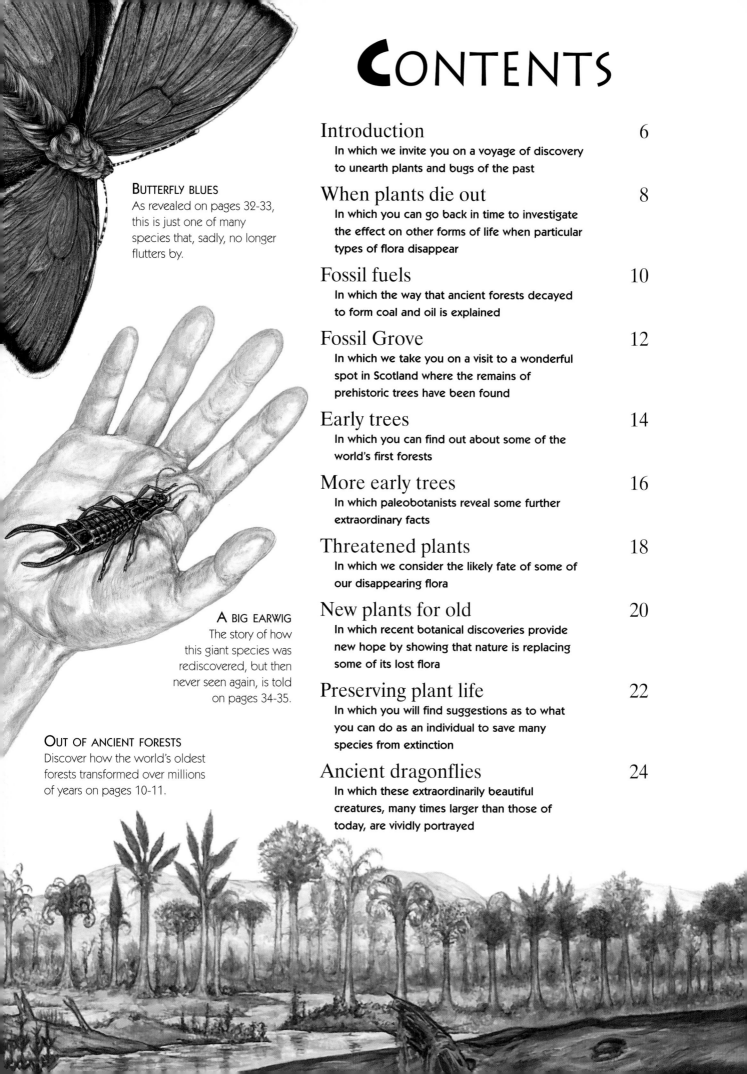

BUTTERFLY BLUES
As revealed on pages 32-33, this is just one of many species that, sadly, no longer flutters by.

A BIG EARWIG
The story of how this giant species was rediscovered, but then never seen again, is told on pages 34-35.

OUT OF ANCIENT FORESTS
Discover how the world's oldest forests transformed over millions of years on pages 10-11.

CONTENTS

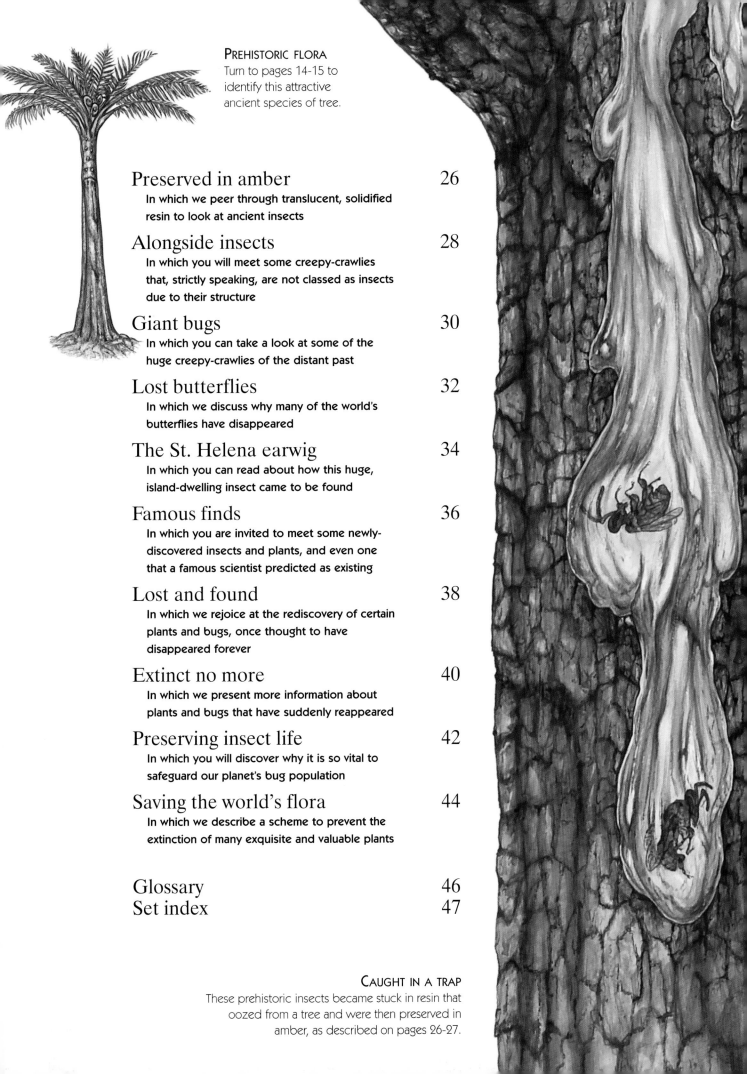

PREHISTORIC FLORA
Turn to pages 14-15 to
identify this attractive
ancient species of tree.

CAUGHT IN A TRAP
These prehistoric insects became stuck in resin that
oozed from a tree and were then preserved in
amber, as described on pages 26-27.

INTRODUCTION

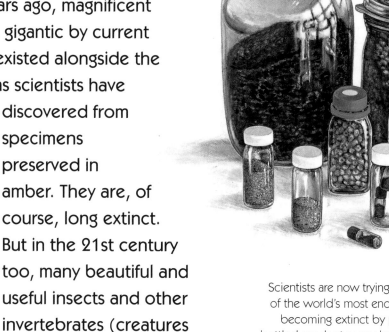

Millions of years ago, magnificent dragonflies, gigantic by current standards, existed alongside the dinosaurs, as scientists have discovered from specimens preserved in amber. They are, of course, long extinct. But in the 21st century too, many beautiful and useful insects and other invertebrates (creatures without backbones) are fast disappearing.

BRAZILIAN BIG BEETLE
This magnificent giant beetle was once believed extinct but has now been rediscovered in Brazil. Not only is it the biggest of its species, it is also the rarest.

BOTTLE BANK
Scientists are now trying to avoid some of the world's most endangered plants becoming extinct by preserving their bottled seeds at a very low temperature.

AN EASTER SURPRISE
Botanists are now trying to revive an acacia tree which died out on Easter Island, site of the famous mysterious statues shown *below*.

Butterflies, such as the marsh fritillary and Camberwell beauty of Europe, for example, have now died out completely. Excessive use of insecticides is often to blame, as are changes in natural habitat due to such factors as drainage of wetlands for farming and deforestation. The overcollecting of specimens introduces a risk factor too. Alternatively, a tree or flower may become extinct when the creature originally responsible for its pollination disappears. When some of Hawaii's beautiful honeycreeper birds began to die out, for instance, a flowering tree, the *Kuahiwi* (<u>KOO</u>-AH-<u>HEE</u>-WEE), soon died out. Similarly, the fate of the dodo, a flightless bird, coincided with failure of new *Calvaria major* or dodo trees to grow.

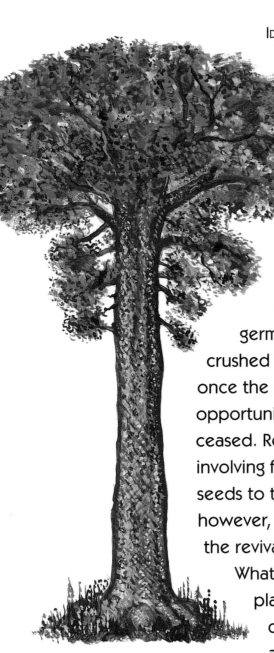

The relationship between the bird and this tree seems to have been a symbiotic one. The seeds would only germinate if the dodo crushed the outer casing; and so once the dodos died out, opportunities for germination ceased. Recent experiments involving force-feeding of the seeds to turkeys are promising, however, so that we yet may see the revival of this tree.

A CITY'S STUMPS
At a place called Fossil Grove in Scotland, several fossilized tree stumps have been preserved in the center of the modern city of Glasgow.

What then could be done, at least in theory, to save other plants and insects from extinction? Flowers should, of course, never be picked unless found in abundance; and conservationists are currently introducing special schemes to ensure the survival of the 20,000 rare plants that are currently endangered worldwide. Read on to find out more.

OUT OF ALL PROPORTION
Its fossils show that the giant prehistoric centipede of Carboniferous times, *below*, 12 inches long, was far larger than any centipede today. It was also highly poisonous.

WHEN PLANTS DIE OUT

When an asteroid hit the Earth 65 million years ago, and sunlight was obscured by all the dust thrown up on impact, most plant life dwindled. Herbivores starved, and there was nothing left for meat-eating dinosaurs either – the result, a mass extinction.

VICIOUS CIRCLE
When species, such as the moth orchid, *right*, become extinct, others of the family fetch higher prices among collectors, so that more of them are taken, and they in turn become rarer.

Animals that have evolved to become entirely dependent on particular plant species for their food intake will inevitably be severely affected if that plant species goes into decline. Take some species of bat, for example. The Jamaican long-tongued variety vanished at the beginning of the 20th century after the loss of the only fruit tree from which it ate.

Similarly, some types of honeycreepers disappeared altogether from Hawaii due to deforestation and the resulting loss of any food supplies for these birds. Granted, many fed on insects, but plant nectar also formed an important part of their diet. In turn, the honeycreepers had assisted with the pollination of certain plants and trees, so that their destiny became intertwined.

DEAD WOOD
The photograph, *right,* of a petrified stump reminds us how important it is to look after the world's trees.

DEAD AS A DODO?
Seeds of the dodo tree, *left*, once germinated by and named after the extinct bird, are now being force-fed to turkeys on Mauritius, so this rare species may perhaps sprout once more.

WHY SAVE PAPER?
Recycling waste paper can help to prevent unnecessary felling of trees, the first stage in its manufacture.

LOST MATES

But sometimes it is the disappearance of just the male or the female of a flower-bearing *dioecious* (<u>DEYE</u>-EE-<u>SHAS</u>) tree – that is, a species whose male and female flowers blossom on different trees – that inevitably leads to the extinction of an entire species. Even if there is one surviving male or female specimen, it may be too old to be grafted successfully. This was the case with a species of black ebony from Mauritius, for example, of which finally only one very old female tree remained.

So what do you think might happen if more species of plants died out? Some food sources might become depleted. But there could be other effects too. If carnivorous plants became extinct, for instance, the insects they previously attracted with the promise of nectar but then entrapped and digested might survive to spread disease or do untold damage. If all the lichens in the world disappeared, scientists would have to find some other way of monitoring the amount of pollution in the atmosphere. If there were no longer suitable trees in the rain forests of India, how would certain species of ants find leaves from which to weave their nests? Without the dead wood of a fallen tree, millions of longhorn beetle larvae might never find the right sort of environment in which to mature, and wasps would not be able to build their paper nests. The effects of loss of plant life are undeniably many and varied.

Fact file

● When plants go extinct, any herbivores that depend mainly on those species as a food source may be seriously affected so that they, too, go into swift decline.

● It may seem strange because some of these delicious fruits are plentiful on the supermarket shelves, but among the most endangered trees and plants today are particular species of olive, date, pomegranate, and avocado, for example.

● *Gaia* (<u>GEYE</u> AH) is the name of a theory concerning what is thought to be the Earth's ability to correct imbalances. But if an entire plant species becomes totally extinct, without its seeds there is no way that it can be brought back into existence.

BIG AND SMELLY
How sad to lose a plant as bizarre as the rafflesia, *below*, the world's largest, rarest, and most strongly-smelling! Botanists are therefore trying to find a way of cultivating it.

Fossil fuel

Coal – like oil and natural gas – is a "fossil fuel," which means it is derived from prehistoric remains and can be burned to release energy. These fossils were formed deep in the earth as layers of rock crushed ancient plant and animal material into something new.

It may be difficult at first to make the link between green plants and a lump of coal, but enormous changes occurred to such vegetation over many millions of years as it became fossilized. Indeed, this type of fuel started to form about 300 million years ago during Carboniferous times, or the so-called "coal age."

Some scientists have suggested that all the Earth's coal was formed as a result of a worldwide flood. But dinosaur footprints and tree remains have been found centrally in coal seams, which proves that the formation of coal must have taken place over a very long period of time.

Oil is another type of fuel created over millions of years from fossilized material – not ancient plants, however, but prehistoric sea creatures.

BURIED SUNSHINE
Coal is often called "buried sunshine" because the plants which long ago formed it captured their energy from the Sun.

REJECTED TREASURE
Fossils of plants, such as the tree fern, *above*, which formed coal have often been thrown out by miners in the shale they discard.

FROM CARBONIFEROUS TIMES
These fossilized seeds are 300 million years old, and the trees from which they came have long turned into coal deposits.

The bodies of these dead organisms sank beneath the oceans, where the action of bacteria, high temperatures, and pressure from above once more turned the remains into a fuel – the thick, viscous substance we know as oil.

Natural gas, meanwhile, comes from the remains of ancient microscopic plants – *phyloplankton* (FEYEL-OH-PLANK-TON) – that still exist today. Over millions of years they decomposed into natural gas which is now retrieved from thousands of feet under the ocean and from some land-based wells.

Nontoxic, the cleanest burning fuel of all, and therefore a current favorite, natural gas can provide more energy than wood, oil, or coal. It has even been calculated that if all the natural gas pipelines in the United States alone were laid end to end, they would extend to over one million miles – a greater distance than from Earth to the Moon!

Fact file

● American geologists divide Carboniferous times into two main epochs – the Mississippian, which came first, and the Pennsylvanian.

● Coal and oil reserves will certainly run dry, so we shall need to start using other renewable sources of energy for heating and various forms of transport.

● Scientists estimate it may have taken up to 10 feet of buried plant matter to create just one foot of coal, due to the way it became compacted during fossilization.

● Laws concerning the use of smokeless fuel in the home and by industry have been passed in many parts of the world in the attempt to prevent pollution of the atmosphere.

BURNING ISSUES
The coal, oil, and natural gas we have today are all formed from ancient fossilized plant and animal organisms. But some coal contains sulfur and when it burns, it pollutes the air. Oil refineries, like the one shown here, can also cause pollution. Natural gas is therefore favored by most conservationists as the most preferable form of fuel.

FOSSIL GROVE

Glasgow in Scotland is a thriving modern city. This makes it all the more surprising that among its main attractions is a group of fossilized trees. Way back in prehistoric times these were part of a huge tropical forest that became devastated by a flood.

A visit to Scotland's Fossil Grove is like taking a trip back in time – so far back, in fact, that you can see the fossilized remains of huge trees that were alive 100 million years before dinosaurs had even started to evolve. But how were they discovered?

In 1887, as a quarry was being dug up to build a local park, workers uncovered some prehistoric remains. One corner of the area therefore became known as Fossil Grove and is a small part of what, 330 million years ago, was a large tropical forest.

SPECTACULAR PLANT
The clubmoss, *right*, was one of the most impressive trees from the coal age. You can see a more detailed depiction of it on page 14.

GIANT STUMPS
There are eight large tree stumps in Fossil Grove and three smaller ones. The tallest, *below*, is three feet in height and has been preserved together with its roots.

LEAF SCARS
The diamond-shaped patterns, *above*, mark where small roots were once attached to the *Lepidodendron* tree.

CAREFUL EXCAVATION
After the site was uncovered, the local authorities decided to build a shelter over the fossils to protect them from being damaged by cold weather.

Fact file

- The trees in Scotland's Fossil Grove date from around 330 million years ago during Carboniferous times, also known as the coal age.

- The exceptionally large clubmoss *Lepidodendron* grew to about 100 feet in height and measured up to 6 feet in diameter.

- The *Lepidodendron* tree was not made of solid wood. It had a strong outer layer of bark, inside which was a thin column of wood protected by a far softer material.

- The trees in Fossil Grove lived so long ago that dinosaurs had not yet appeared on Earth. Spiders, scorpions, and insects were the most common creatures in what is now Scotland at that time.

FROM THE COAL AGE
The central feature of the area is a group of 11 fossilized tree stumps, the remains of a species of primitive clubmoss known as a *Lepidodendron* (LEP-ID-OH-<u>DEN</u>-DRON). Clubmosses are some of the first land plants to have appeared on the Earth and were common during Carboniferous times which lasted from 360 to 286 million years ago. A distinctive scar made by their leaves and found on the small remnant of a branch helped scientists identify the stumps as those of the *Lepidodendrons*.

BOMB DAMAGE
The remains can be seen in a special fossil house, opened in 1890. However, after surviving for so long, one of the stumps was damaged by a bomb during World War II and had to be repaired with concrete.

NATURAL CASTS
The fossilized tree stumps are made from sandstone – none of the original tree material survives. Long ago, the forest where the trees lived was flooded and the trees died. Their upper parts broke off and floated away, and the soft interiors of the trees rotted, leaving just the bark. They then became buried in sand, which also filled up the hollow interiors of the stumps.

Over a long period of time the sand hardened to become sandstone, so what we see today are sandstone casts of the original trunks. The stumps are also no longer circular but angled to one side due to the effects of the flooding.

FALLEN TRUNK
The remains of a giant clubmoss lie near the stumps of Fossil Grove. The 27-foot-long tree trunk was carried to its present position by flood waters.

EARLY TREES

Who would have thought it might be possible to grow seeds from a 200-million-year-old pine discovered near Sydney, Australia, in 1994! How have botanists managed to achieve this?

What fun to grow a tree in your garden that dates back to the age of the dinosaurs! It may sound unlikely but this will soon be possible thanks to the chance discovery of a tree known as the Wollemi pine.

It all began in 1994, when a park ranger spotted a group of about 40 strange trees in the Wollemi National Park near Sydney, Australia. Examination showed its closest relatives were pine trees dating from Jurassic and Cretaceous times.

The Wollemi pine grows to a height of 120 feet and can live for hundreds of years. Its Latin name, *Wollemi nobilis* (WO-LEHM-EE NOH-BIL-IS) comes from the combination of an aboriginal word, *Wollemia*, meaning "look around you" and the name of the park ranger, David Noble.

GROW YOUR OWN

Seeds were taken from this ancient tree's cones, and local botanists hope to make them available to the public. Huge demand is expected as the tree can grow in many different types of climate. It also has beautiful pale green leaves and a fascinating knobbly bark, described as looking like bubbling chocolate.

KNOWN BY TWO NAMES
The *Calamites* (KAL-AM-EYE-TEEZ), *left,* was a giant horsetail which grew from an underground rhizome (REYE-ZOHM) as far back as Carboniferous times. Its name refers only to cast fossils of its stem. Fossils of its leaves are called *Annularia* (AN-YOOL-AR-EE-AH).

CLUB MEMBER
The gigantic clubmoss shown *left* had a very long, slim trunk and four principal roots which then became subdivided into Y-shaped rootlets. Fossilized remains show that part of its bark had a well-defined, scalelike pattern. Known as a *Lepidodendron* (LEP-ID-OH-DEN-DRON), it stood up to 130 feet in height and grew in hot and humid swamplands back in Carboniferous times which lasted from 345-280 million years ago.

TURNED TO COAL

The *Psaronius* (<u>SAR</u>-OHN-EE-US) shown here was a tree fern. All the way up its slim trunk was a layer of fibrous rootlets. It was one of the many trees of the Carboniferous forests which have given us coal.

Meanwhile, the trees' exact location in the vast Wollemi National Park has been kept a complete secret for fear that collectors might steal cuttings or seeds from the few living examples.

A NEW DAWN

This is not the only early tree thought to have become extinct but making an appearance again in the 20th century. At one time trees known as dawn redwoods were to be found all over the world but, due to lack of fossil evidence, they were thought to have died out 20 million years ago – until, that is, a group of them suddenly turned up in the mountains of central China during the 1940s.

The dawn redwood, or *Metasequoia* (<u>MET</u>-AH-SEK-<u>OI</u>-YAH), is related to the giant redwoods of California, the world's tallest trees. But there is one big difference.

Unlike the giant redwoods, the dawn redwoods are deciduous. This means they shed their leaves each fall. They are not quite as old as the Wollemi pine, but still date back millions of years to Jurassic times, when the sauropod dinosaurs were in their prime.

The history of the dawn redwood captured the imagination of botanists, and seeds were taken from this 200-foot-high ancient tree's cones with the result that it is now found once more right around the world. We are, of course, lucky to have two such splendid trees still with us; but the most ancient of all are only known from fossil records. The very earliest, seed ferns and horsetails among them, evolved some 300 million years ago and were well suited to the swamps of Carboniferous times. Some are illustrated across these two pages.

SWAMP LOVER

This *Medullosa* (<u>MED</u>-UL-<u>OH</u>-SAH) tree was a seed fern, growing up to 16 feet in height. It was typical of those plants found in Carboniferous swamps of what is now the United States.

Fact file

● When the Wollemi pine first flourished, Australia was part of the giant supercontinent, Gondwana, which included what is now Africa, South America, and India. Only later did this land mass split apart.

● True conifers (cone-bearing trees such as pines, firs, and spruces) prefer dry conditions and so did not become widespread until after the end of damp and swampy Carboniferous times.

● Dinosaurs probably reared up on their hind legs to feed from the tallest early trees.

● Dawn redwoods can grow as much as six feet in a year. This helped them survive damage caused by plant-eating creatures, such as the sauropod dinosaurs.

MORE EARLY TREES

The oldest known living tree species, according to legend, was saved from extinction by a group of Chinese monks who preserved specimens in their garden. Today, ten million of these ancient trees can be found growing in South Carolina.

In 1991 ship's captain Peter Lindquist was sailing on Lake Superior, the deepest of the five great lakes of North America, when he happened to notice a strange reading on one of his ship's instruments. Deep in the waters below, there appeared to be two tall masts poking up from the seabed. Thinking they might have belonged to a sunken ship, Lindquist and a colleague swiftly put on their diving gear and went to have a look. They even wondered whether there was buried treasure to be found. The objects, however, proved not to be ships' masts but upright, fossilized trees.

There were five in all, each about 20 feet in height. So how had they got there? Thousands of years ago, during an Ice Age when water levels were lower than they are today, they had been growing on the shores of what is now Lake Superior. Now, however, they were part of a sunken, prehistoric grove.

Many species of trees failed to survive the conditions of the world's several Ice Ages, just as a great number perished in the mass extinction that wiped out the dinosaurs and many other plant and animal species at the end of Cretaceous times.

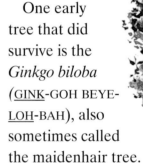

One early tree that did survive is the *Ginkgo biloba* (<u>GINK</u>-GOH BEYE-<u>LOH</u>-BAH), also sometimes called the maidenhair tree. The first part of its name comes from a Chinese word meaning "silver apricot," and the tree's seed does indeed look like one. *Biloba,* meanwhile, means "two-lobed," as its leaf has a division down its middle. Its earliest fossils date back 270 million years and, by the time of the dinosaurs, it was a common tree with many varieties.

WEIRD AND WIDESPREAD
The illustration, *left,* is a reconstruction of what paleobotanists think a very unusually shaped tree, the *Nilssonia* (NIL-<u>SOHN</u>-EE-AH), would have looked like. It is thought to have been very common in many parts of the world in Jurassic times.

TALL TREE
The huge Jurassic sauropods would have found it easy to browse on trees such as the *Classopolis, left,* a conifer growing to 40 feet in height. Pollen has even been collected from its ancient remains.

GROUND COVER
Small ferns were prolific in Jurassic times, providing ground cover under the trees and in open areas instead of grass, which only appeared 100 million years ago.

HEALING TREE

The ginkgo's leaves are said to improve blood circulation, aid memory loss, and protect against heart disease and strokes, for example.

This tree's leaves are fan-shaped; and the male tree produces pollen in hanging spikes, while the female grows ovules that are the size of a cherry and contain a large pip.

Today, the largest ginkgo plantation in the world is in Sumter, South Carolina, where around ten million of these trees are grown for their medicinal value.

When dinosaurs ruled the world back in Mesozoic times, the landscape was dominated by ginkgos, conifers, horsetails, ferns, and cycads, some of which are shown on these two pages.

But the ginkgo gradually declined in numbers to the point where it was considered extinct – until, that is, ginkgos were rediscovered in 1691 by a German botanist working in Japan. Its seeds were then brought to Europe, and it is now grown as an ornamental tree all over the world.

However, the ginkgo is more than just a "living fossil." The Japanese and Chinese have long eaten its nuts and seeds, as well as using them to cure ailments, while western medicine has more recently discovered a number of important uses for the ginkgo's leaves.

Fact file

- *Gingko biloba* extract is an herb made from the leaves of that tree. Today, it is the most frequently prescribed herbal medicine in Germany and France.

- The ginkgo occupies a unique position among trees and is often thought of as a link between ferns and conifers.

- One ginkgo tree in China is said to be 3,500 years old.

- Seed plants are called gymnosperms, meaning "naked seeds," because they are not enclosed in a fruit but are protected by cones or a fleshy seed coat.

- The Mesozoic era is also called the "age of cycads," so successful was this seed plant in spreading across the world at that time.

All these trees provided excellent feeding grounds for herbivores. Indeed, those that fed on the ginkgo must have benefited from its valuable, health-giving properties.

FROM THE TOP
Small, plant-eating dinosaurs probably often ate leaves sprouting from the top of pineapple-shaped cycads (SEYE-KADZ), such as the one shown here.

THREATENED PLANTS

Throughout the world there are places where exquisite indigenous plants are becoming severely endangered for a whole variety of reasons. Even particular strains of otherwise very common plants are now rare. Some are presented across these two pages.

Many of the mangrove trees of the Philippines are currently no more than dead trunks, standing beside a ruined ecosystem, due to deforestation and the clearing of swamps that once formed their natural habitat to provide suitable conditions for fish farming.

Several schemes now exist on the islands to protect both animals and plants, however, and these actively encourage tree planting.

In the West Indies and South America, meanwhile, plants called *epiphytes* (EP-EE-FEYETS) face an equally serious threat.

LOST BEAUTY
The echium plant, very rare in the Canary Islands off Africa, is seen in flower in the photograph, *above*.

SEVERELY AT RISK
In the United States one plant in every three is under threat. Among those most at risk are 32% of all irises, *below*, 29% of palms, and 14% of roses.

WILD NO MORE
Monkey puzzle trees, *above*, are now virtually extinct in the wild, but they are found almost exclusively as cultivated plants.

Many species of these climbers, also known as air plants, face extinction principally because far too many have been collected for sale as house plants.

Those orchids that are epiphytes have been most badly hit, notably in Ecuador. At one time orchids were highly numerous and diverse there, but huge areas of rain forest have been cut down for farmland over the last few decades. And on Trinidad, another species of epiphyte, which once thrived high up on the island, has become endangered due to the careless trampling of too many hikers.

PRICKLY PROBLEM

In Texas and regions of Mexico some species of cacti are under threat because this prickly plant is so popular that it is exported to collectors worldwide. Rare cacti are picked illegally by rustlers and then smuggled overseas to be sold for high prices.

UP IN THE MOUNTAINS

In Europe, meanwhile, an increasing number of alpine species are gradually becoming endangered. Indeed, flowering plants in particular have declined in mountainous areas due to use of pesticides and herbicides, as well as the introduction of large numbers of grazing animals.

Mountain walkers who thoughtlessly pick plants already scarce in such regions are clearly at fault, while the skiing industry sometimes causes damage to the natural habitat, leading to a subsequent decline in some alpine species. Even members of the horticultural trade, who should know better, have greedily sought rare specimens. In the end, maybe the only way to safeguard the world's threatened plants will be to introduce a force of plant police, some botanists suggest.

Fact file

● At least one in every eight of the world's known 270,000 plant species is currently under threat of extinction. In the United States, however, the situation is far worse. Here, and it is more like one in three.

● The main reasons why plants and trees become endangered include logging, the crowding out of native species by newly introduced species, and the destruction of natural habitats in favor of farming or building.

● Sometimes, survival of certain plants depends on successful control of local wildlife. One hibiscus species, for example, native to Philip Island in the Pacific Ocean, became endangered due to increase in the rabbit population.

GROWING INTEREST
Many conservationists are now dedicated to planting seedlings of such rare trees as the *Pau-brasil* (POW BRA-SIL), *right.* It became endangered due to devastation of its rain-forest habitat.

NEW PLANTS FOR OLD

Fortunately, as some plants and trees become increasingly endangered or even extinct, botanists continue to find fresh species, breed new varieties artificially, and even introduce some favorites to other regions. But is this always with the desired result?

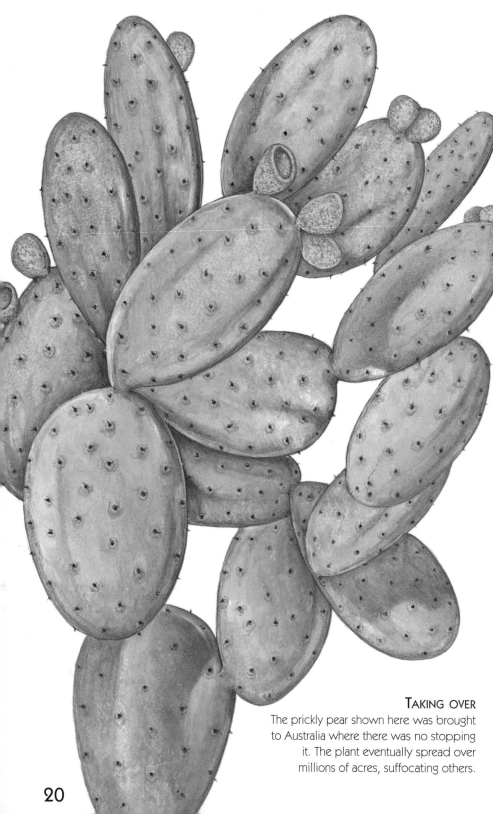

Usually, different species cannot interbreed. But there are exceptions. A tangerine and a grapefruit tree can give rise to the so-called ugli fruit, for instance.

This is an example of a hybrid (HEYE-BRID), the result of breeding two different but related species, or two varieties of one species. Sometimes it occurs naturally over a long period of time.

GROWING APART

Hybrids may appear, for instance, when two groups of a species become separated from each other, perhaps following the breaking up of land to form new islands, the melting of polar ice caps, or the growth of mountains.

Each group may then have to adapt to new conditions while separated by what scientists refer to as an "isolating mechanism." They may face differing weather conditions, for instance, or competition from surrounding species, and so adapt accordingly. Depending on what changes they face and the time for which they are separated, the two plant populations may be able to breed if brought back together again either by chance or intentionally. Alternatively, they may evolve into two entirely distinct species that are no longer able to breed.

NATIONAL EMBLEM
This orchid from the Costa Rican rain forest is its national flower but has become endangered. Will they therefore one day need to choose a replacement?

Fact file

● Crops are thought to owe about 50% of their increased productivity today to the making of hybrids (*hybridization*) and the use of selective breeding programs developed by agriculturalists.

● In the 1970s, a virus threatened to stunt the growth of a type of rice grown all over Asia, on which many millions of people were entirely reliant for food. The International Rice Institute therefore bred a disease-resistant hybrid which is now widely grown.

● Geographical speciation (SPEE-SHEE-AY-SHON) is the term used to describe how hybrids may occur when a species becomes separated by a geographical feature and each group then adapts to prevailing conditions.

This is what happened with a type of grass, some of which became exposed to poisonous metals dumped in an area of North Wales. After a while, it was found the original seeds were no longer able to breed with the new, stronger variety. A hybrid had evolved as a response to changing conditions. But horticulturalists also breed hybrids to combine the best characteristics of each parent plant.

In most cases such artificial intervention is aimed at changing a plant's appearance, or increasing its yield and improving its taste, in the case of crops. Farmers may also want to develop a hybrid that is more resistant to disease and faster growing.

Often a lot of trial and error is involved as unwanted traits may reappear long after they were thought to have been eradicated. And a number of scientists admit there could be a definite downside. Indeed, many people now actively campaign against genetically modified foods, fearing they may not be totally safe. It is an area of great controversy.

BRED BY BOTANISTS
This magnificent flower – a spooned variety of African daisy – is a hybrid, bred from different species of the plant.

BETTER CROPS
The variety of rice, shown in flower in the photograph *below*, has been developed for an improved yield and quality for the population of Bangladesh.

PRESERVING PLANT LIFE

A MATTER OF SURVIVAL
Through careful study of rare specimens in their natural habitat, as shown *above*, botanists can discover more about the needs of particular plant species.

A Hindu sect based in India and dating back to the 15th century was formed after a villager had a vision of humans bringing disaster on themselves by maltreating nature. Today, too, they consider it a duty to protect not only trees and plants but animal life as well.

According to a great sage of India, trees give us ten valuable things. These are oxygen, water, energy, food, clothes, timber, medicinal herbs, fodder, flowers, and shade. That country has certainly long appreciated the importance of environmental conservation. In 1730, for example, more than 350 women gave their lives in the attempt to save trees.

A local ruler had ordered several to be cut down but the women refused to let it happen, and it is said they perished by the sword as they embraced the threatened trees.

More recently, in 1973 a group known as the Chipko Movement was established in India and has since proved true to its name, meaning "hold fast." Indeed, when forest trees were due to be taken for industry village women behaved in exactly the same way as those who had once been martyrs for a similar cause, except that this time their efforts proved successful and the trees were saved.

GREEN REVOLUTION

In Europe, too, there have long been visionaries when it came to the importance of plant conservation. Way back in the 4th century B.C., for example, the philosopher Plato warned his fellow Greeks of the dangers to plant and animal life if the practice of cutting down forests on the hillsides around Athens was allowed to continue, but to no avail. The results can now be seen in the eroded, barren landscape surrounding their capital city.

In modern times most people would not go so far as to risk their lives for the sake of conservation. But from time to time, bands of so-called eco-warriors take matters so seriously that they will even demonstrate by climbing trees about to be felled on land designated for redevelopment. Such extremists usually remain in the treetops until physically removed by the law enforcers.

CACTUS CRIME
Whenever botanists find the beautiful flowering Knowlton's cactus, *left*, they do everything they can to protect and tend it, since it is extremely endangered due to illegal collection and export.

KEEPING IN TOUCH
Some people believe talking to your plants, hugging trees just as the boy in this illustration is doing, and even playing soft classical music to them can encourage growth. But a lot more positive action is required to preserve plants that have become endangered.

There are, however, lots of other things the concerned among us can do to prevent unnecessary loss of plant life. We can, for example, take part in environmental education programs; visit botanical gardens or an arboretum (tree collection) to increase our appreciation of plant life; perhaps join volunteers in clearing areas so polluted that the local flora is becoming suffocated; or even, as adults, assist a recognized organization overseas with reintroduction of vegetation after a drought.

We can and should do everything possible to reduce the greenhouse effect, also known as global warming, thereby saving delicate plants from becoming exposed to unsuitable climatic conditions so that they go into gradual decline. (Take a look at another volume in this set, *Why Extinction Occurs*, for further information on this topic.) Buy recycled paper whenever possible too, bearing in mind that no further trees will have been chopped down to provide what you need.

Fact file

● Botanists suggest we should never pick wild flowers. There is always a danger we might accidentally uproot an endangered species.

● Scientists have calculated that part of California contains 25% of all plant species found in North America; and over 2,000 species (or 50% of plants growing in this area) are found nowhere else in the world. Sadly, their natural habitat is rapidly being restricted due to urban development and the clearing of land for agricultural use.

● A World Conservation Strategy has been prepared in association with scientists and local people from all over the globe. Its aim is to save the many species of our green world for future generations.

And finally, we can ask ourselves what we can do about *us*, since the human species has been ultimately responsible for the demise of so much plant life. What can we do to influence other citizens and those in power so that they sit up and take notice? If nothing is done, paleobotanists of the distant future will not doubt explain to our descendants that humans of the 21st century were mostly negligent in their attitude to plant conservation.

ANCIENT DRAGONFLIES

The ancestors of today's dragonflies were, on average, about five times their current size. In fact, one such prehistoric dragonfly, whose remains have been found in North America and Europe, may well have been the largest of all the world's insects.

The most extraordinary thing about the prehistoric dragonfly known as *Meganeura* (MEG-AN-YOOR-AH) was its wingspan which extended to as much as 30 inches. Today's biggest dragonfly with a wingspan of only seven-and-a-half inches is tiny in comparison.

Members of the insect order Odonata (OH-DON-AH-TAH), dragonflies have probably always been fast-flying creatures with powerful jaws. Indeed, the word Odonata means "toothed ones," and the common name "dragonfly" was selected because their mouthparts resemble those of the mythical dragon.

TURNED TO STONE
Many remains of *Meganeura* have been found in Pennsylvania, as well as England and France. Their fossils are numerous because these insects very often fell into soft mud or sand at the bottom of the ponds and lakes that once formed their natural habitat. As more soft material was then added, the pressure of the water or ground above these remains slowly turned them into long-lasting stone.

Meganeura was large, its size only limited by its ability to draw enough oxygen through its body to power the muscles used to flap its wings. In other words, this dragonfly seems to have grown as big as its basic bodily design would allow.

Present-day dragonflies are prey to birds (including ducks), lizards, frogs, fish, and even some spiders. But in prehistoric times, before the first reptiles had evolved on Earth, these large dragonflies had few rivals or enemies and were rarely attacked or eaten by insectivores. Only when the first, small dinosaurs appeared were the lives of ancient dragonflies ever really at risk.

JURASSIC GIANT
This cute, fossilized dragonfly is about 140 million years old and was unearthed in Bavaria, Germany.

As for their own feeding habits, today's dragonflies are very active predators and there is no reason to think their ancient relatives were different.

In fact, as they do now, they probably ate almost anything available, including flies and other insects (even other dragonflies), and also tadpoles and fish.

SIGHT AND FLIGHT
Two natural advantages would have helped these prehistoric insects when it came to feeding – their magnificent aerial skills and their superb eyesight. Just like the dragonflies of today, they had thousands of lenses in their big eyes, which not only gave a very wide field of vision but helped them to see far into the distance too.

No one is sure exactly how fast *Meganeura* could fly, but paleontologists think it could move considerably more rapidly than even the speediest modern dragonfly, which is known to zoom along at an amazing 35 miles per hour.

However, they may not have been as agile in the air as the far smaller, modern family members. Dragonflies of today can twist and turn, flapping their wings at the rate of 40 times per second. Larger wings, though fine in structure, may have been more unwieldy. In any event, like dragonflies of today, those of the past are unlikely to have moved far from the watercourses where they were born.

ON THE WING
Meganeura's wingspan extended to about 30 inches. The modern world has seen nothing like it.

Fact file

- Dragonflies have existed on this planet for well over 350 million years, but no one knows from which creatures they evolved.

- Those prehistoric insects that were far bigger than their present-day counterparts are sometimes referred to as macro-invertebrates.

- Some modern species of dragonflies are threatened with extinction by humans who build over and destroy their natural habitat. In fact, over 100 different species of dragonflies are thought to be endangered, according to the International Union for the Conservation of Nature.

- Japan was the first country in the world to create a dragonfly nature reserve.

The largest prehistoric dragonflies probably died out when environmental conditions changed and with the appearance of pterosaurs, flying reptiles that had started to evolve by Triassic times. The pterosaurs were certainly well adapted to catching and feeding on even the largest prehistoric insects.

25

PRESERVED IN AMBER

If you have seen the movie *Jurassic Park* or read the book, you will know the story is about a group of scientists who create a sensational dinosaur park on a remote Pacific island with the help of amber. But what exactly is this substance?

Yellow-orange in color and translucent, amber is a precious commodity today and frequently used to make jewelry. So who would have thought that millions of years ago it was simply a sweet, sticky liquid exuding from under the bark of trees to which early insects were frequently attracted! When this substance (resin) dried, insects sometimes became stuck in it; and once it hardened into amber, they were well and truly trapped.

Most of the world's amber now comes from two distinct areas. One is the Dominican Republic in the Caribbean; the other is the Baltic, a region of eastern Europe.

The amber from these places also came from different trees. In the Dominican Republic, the tree responsible was the *Hymenaea protera* (HIM-EN-EYE-AH PRO-TER-AH). This tree is now extinct but related species still exist in the West Indies and Africa. In the Baltic, meanwhile, amber came from an extinct pinelike tree known as the *Pinites succinifer* (PEYE-NEYE-TEEZ SOOK-IN-IF-ER). Both grew in what were sub-tropical climates at the time. Present-day relatives of the trees that once produced amber still produce some resin, but this tends to break down into other substances and does not ever transform into amber.

Most amber started to form during the Carboniferous period, and paleontologists believe the resin from which it was formed may have been exuded for any one of several reasons. It could, for instance, have been a form of protection against fungal attack.

ADDED VALUE
A piece of amber jewelry containing a fossilized prehistoric spider and cricket, *above*, will have special significance for someone interested in paleontology.

In some circumstances it may even have been a part of the tree's growth process, or a method of attracting insects to help pollination.

HEALING SUBSTANCE
However, most experts believe the most common reason for resin production was to protect against external damage, especially harm caused by any insects who bored their way into the tree. Resin would then be produced from within the tree's wood to fill the hole as a method of self-healing.

From leaves and other plant substances found in amber, scientists have learned much about the make-up of Carboniferous forests. Indeed, remains of ancient trees including junipers, beeches, oaks, willows, laurels, and maples have all been found.

NO ESCAPE
The photograph, *left*, shows a gall gnat which became fossilized in Baltic amber about 30 million years ago. You can see patterns made as it struggled to get free.

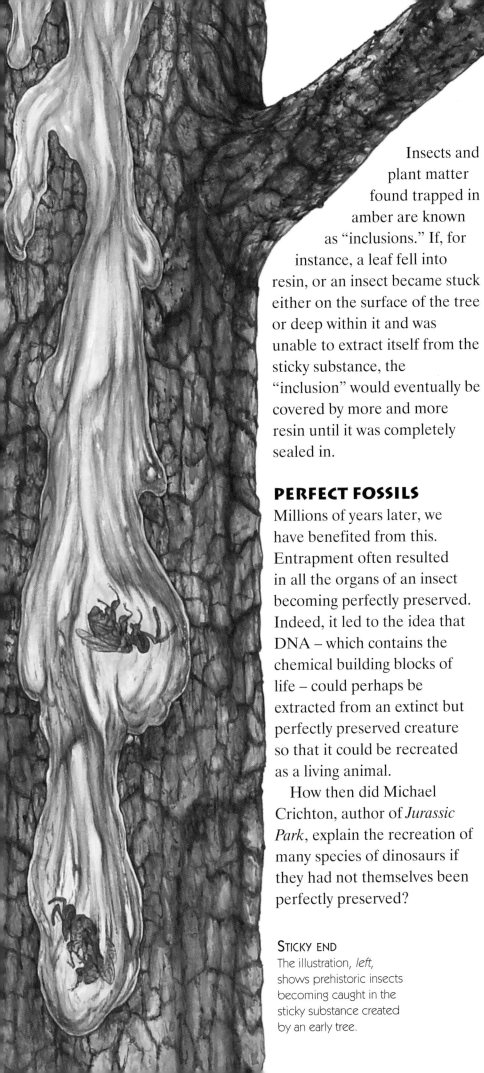

Insects and plant matter found trapped in amber are known as "inclusions." If, for instance, a leaf fell into resin, or an insect became stuck either on the surface of the tree or deep within it and was unable to extract itself from the sticky substance, the "inclusion" would eventually be covered by more and more resin until it was completely sealed in.

PERFECT FOSSILS

Millions of years later, we have benefited from this. Entrapment often resulted in all the organs of an insect becoming perfectly preserved. Indeed, it led to the idea that DNA – which contains the chemical building blocks of life – could perhaps be extracted from an extinct but perfectly preserved creature so that it could be recreated as a living animal.

How then did Michael Crichton, author of *Jurassic Park*, explain the recreation of many species of dinosaurs if they had not themselves been perfectly preserved?

STICKY END
The illustration, *left*, shows prehistoric insects becoming caught in the sticky substance created by an early tree.

Fact file

● One very rich site for amber is a place called La Toca in the Dominican Republic. Here, miners frequently come across insects and spiders that became fossilized in sticky resin or sap many millions of years ago.

● Resins were produced from within certain trees – mostly pines and gymnosperms – if they were damaged.

● Baltic amber, from Russia and other countries in that region, is especially highly valued for its quality.

● Amber has been found in many other places, including Burma (Myanmar), New Zealand, Canada, Japan, Alaska, Germany, Romania, Great Britain, Mexico, Israel, Jordan, and Lebanon.

The important link was a number of amber-trapped mosquitoes. In theory, scientists might have been able to recreate the prehistoric mosquitoes. But in this story they went one enormous step further and reasoned that if the mosquitoes happened to have bitten a dinosaur to enjoy a meal of its blood, a single drop of that blood in each preserved mosquito's gut might contain sufficient DNA to rebuild that species of dinosaur. In reality, scientists have not yet managed to extract dinosaur DNA from ancient insects and recreate these beasts. But it is an area of research and only time will tell.

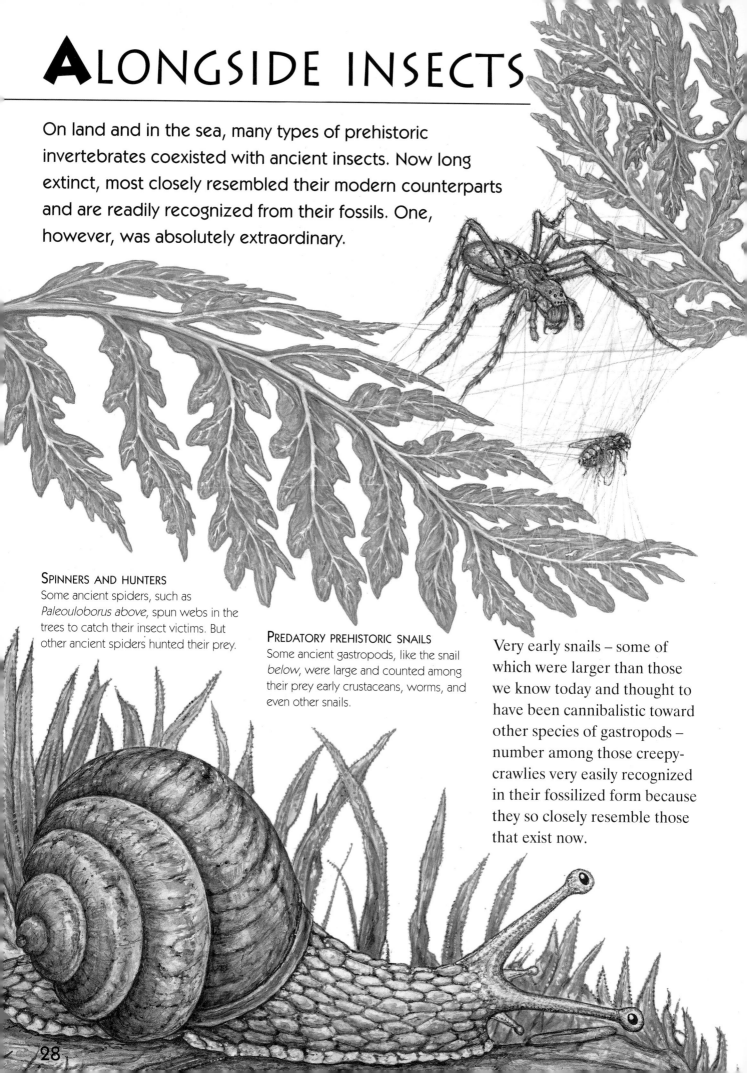

ALONGSIDE INSECTS

On land and in the sea, many types of prehistoric invertebrates coexisted with ancient insects. Now long extinct, most closely resembled their modern counterparts and are readily recognized from their fossils. One, however, was absolutely extraordinary.

SPINNERS AND HUNTERS
Some ancient spiders, such as *Paleouloborus above*, spun webs in the trees to catch their insect victims. But other ancient spiders hunted their prey.

PREDATORY PREHISTORIC SNAILS
Some ancient gastropods, like the snail *below*, were large and counted among their prey early crustaceans, worms, and even other snails.

Very early snails – some of which were larger than those we know today and thought to have been cannibalistic toward other species of gastropods – number among those creepy-crawlies very easily recognized in their fossilized form because they so closely resemble those that exist now.

ANCIENT SPIDERS

Many other types of prehistoric invertebrates have not changed much either. From fossilized remains, for instance, paleontologists know that, over 300 million years ago, there was a highly dangerous spider on our planet, *Arthrolycosa* (ARTH-ROL-IK-OH-SAH.) Like spiders today, *Arthrolycosa* had eight legs so that it is not classed as an insect, which must have six legs. Its other main characteristics were the small claws at the end of its legs which it used to grasp its prey. It also had fangs through which it could inject enough nasty venom to kill a small predator outright, just as some modern spiders do.

Remains of ancient invertebrates are rarely unearthed because many were eaten or lived in environments that were not ideally suited to fossilization. But one fossil of a tiny spider known as *Paleouloborus* (PAL-EE-OH-UL-OH-BOR-US) is so perfectly preserved that it is possible to see not only its fangs but the miniature spinnerets which must have manufactured delicate thread for its web.

From trace fossils found of other early spiders, meanwhile, we know that way back in time they lived in shallow swamps or lagoons, as well as on land.

UPSIDE DOWN?
Scientists were so puzzled at first by the structure of *Hallucigenia's* body that they could not decide which way up its 600-million-year-old fossil should go.

HOW ODD!

But paleontologists have also found ancient invertebrates that are very strange indeed, among them the creature they named *Hallucigenia* (HAL-OOS-IJ-EEN-EE-AH) because it means "unreal." In fact, when they found its fossilized remains in British Columbia, they were truly astonished because it was unlike any other marine creature yet discovered. Its body was tubelike, just over one inch long, with a head at one end and an upturning tail at the other. At first, experts were stumped as to how it moved but now know it had several legs. It also had lots of spikes sticking upward from the top of its body which gave protection against predators. How odd some of our planet's extinct invertebrates were!

Fact file

- No ancient fossilized spiders' webs remain; but we can assume they made them because there is evidence that, like modern spiders, they had spinnerets, organs used for producing the silky thread.

- Spiders probably first appeared in Devonian times, which lasted from 395-345 million years ago.

- Land gastropods (snails) are thought to have first appeared in the Carboniferous forests.

- Worms are rarely preserved as true fossils because they are soft-bodied and very readily disintegrate over time. But they occur as so-called trace fossils – traces or impressions made by their bodies in substances that hardened over many millions of years.

GIANT BUGS

Some of the earliest invertebrates were so well-suited to life on Earth that they have changed very little over hundreds of millions of years – except for their size, that is. A number that are tiny today were once colossal.

Perhaps you have read science fiction in which great big cockroaches eventually take over our planet, gargantuan flies invade the Earth, or man-eating beetles conquer the world. Images such as these can be terrifying and prey on the imagination. They are indeed gross exaggerations. Yet once there actually were species of cockroaches large enough to fight a mouse, flies the size of pigeons, and beetles as long as your arm.

POISONOUS PREDATOR

Back in Carboniferous times, there were 12-inch long centipedes, such as *Latzelia* (<u>LAT</u>-ZEEL-<u>EE</u>-AH) *below*, which killed their prey using poisonous fangs.

In an old mine in Ohio in 2001, geologists even found a 300 million-year-old cockroach fossil almost 3.5 inches long and therefore over twice the size of any modern roach. It dates back to about 55 million years before the dinosaurs had started to evolve, and is about one inch longer than the previous fossilized record-holding roach.

But even though roaches are far smaller today, scientists agree there is no likelihood they will become endangered. Indeed, they are

BIG STINGER

Millions of years ago, scorpions such as *Palaeophonus* (<u>PAL</u>-EYE-OH-<u>FOHN</u>-US), shown here, were over 3 feet long.

thought to be among the hardiest of any creatures on Earth, and possibly capable of surviving a nuclear holocaust.

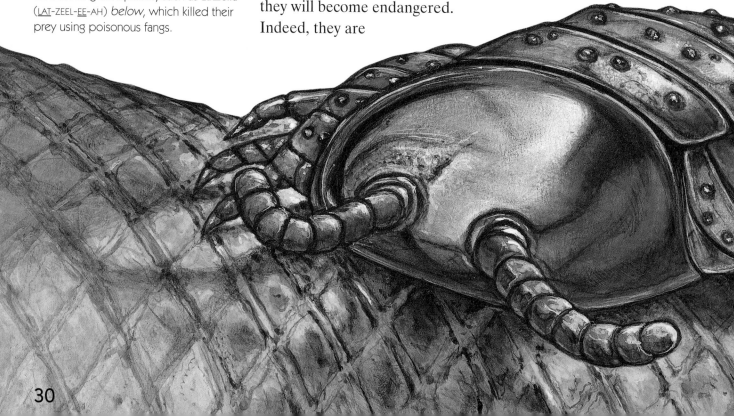

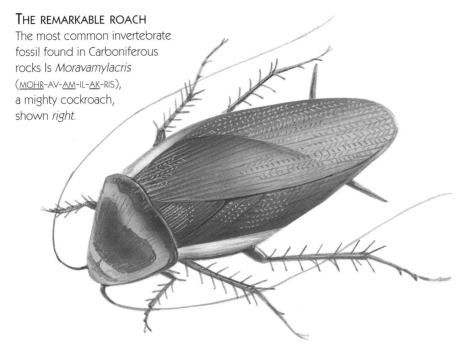

THE REMARKABLE ROACH
The most common invertebrate fossil found in Carboniferous rocks Is *Moravamylacris* (MOHR-AV-AM-IL-AK-RIS), a mighty cockroach, shown *right*.

Fact file

● Hundreds of millions of years ago, no one had to worry about being attacked by giant bugs simply because no humans had yet evolved.

● Fossil evidence shows that the first land animals to have evolved are likely to have been millipedes.

● An arthropod is an animal with a hard body-covering and jointed legs. Insects, centipedes, millipedes, spiders, scorpions, and crustaceans are all arthropods, but worms and snails are not.

● Giant, predatory sea scorpions, such as *Pterygotus* (TER-EE-GOHT-US) inhabited the oceans over 400 million years ago and were about 8 feet in length – as long as a family-sized car.

But that Ohio mine held another big surprise. There the geologists also found the fossil of a creature closely resembling a centipede, but measuring an incredible 5 feet in length instead of just a couple of inches. What, then, could have caused such growth?

According to one new theory, there may have been much more oxygen in the atmosphere in Paleozoic times when these giant bugs thrived.

Analysis of soil samples seems to back the idea that prehistoric plant life produced large amounts of oxygen. Meanwhile, laboratory experiments show that larger insects become more active if given more oxygen than there generally is in the atmosphere today, whereas smaller ones can get by with much less. So perhaps insects had to get smaller over millions of years to survive.

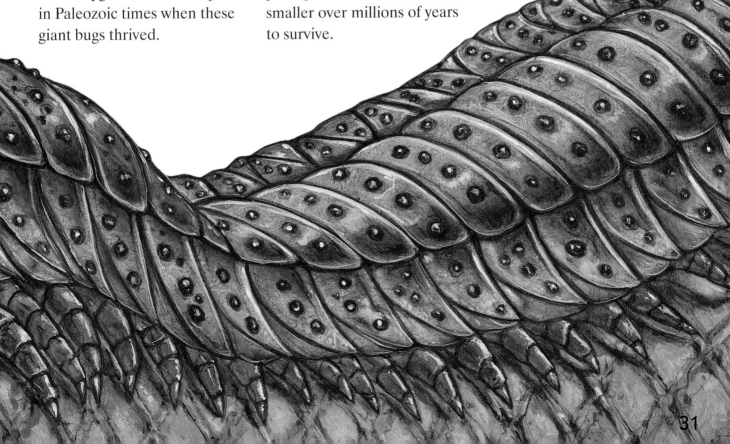

LOST BUTTERFLIES

Butterflies are in peril worldwide due mostly to thoughtless destruction of their natural habitats for economic gain. But serious collectors are partly to blame too and do not seem to realize the terrible effect their hobby has had on a whole variety of endangered butterfly species. Which are the rarest of all today? And what can be done to save these exquisite but very short-lived creatures?

The first North American butterfly to become extinct through human interference was the so-called *Xerces* (ZER-SEES) blue. But the rarest of all butterflies anywhere in the world today is the Queen Alexandra's birdwing, native to the forests of Papua New Guinea. The eruption of a local volcano destroyed much of its natural habitat in 1951; and since then this birdwing, also the world's largest surviving butterfly, has been further threatened by the continual clearing of land for human settlement and for farming.

In the course of its lifetime, a female Queen Alexandra's birdwing may lay over 200 eggs, but by no means all will mature to become butterflies. Some of the tiny eggs may not be viable, or will be taken by predators. The emerging caterpillars are also often eaten by snakes and a variety of other creatures.

LOSING THE BLUES
The Mazarine blue butterfly, *left,* is at risk in North Africa and Asia, and already extinct in parts of Europe. A number of other "blues" are also now extinct on the American continent; but fortunately, as fast as they vanish, others are newly discovered.

Fact file

- Females of the endangered Queen Alexandra's birdwing species have a larger wingspan than the males.

- Many endangered butterfly species have been affected by excessive use of agricultural pesticides.

- Many collectors of butterfly specimens are probably unaware of the effect of their hobby on endangered species.

- Some butterflies rely on such features as warning coloration, camouflage, and mimicry to protect themselves from predators, such as birds.

- Even brightly colored butterflies merge into the background when resting because, unlike moths, they hold their wings together and only the dull underside shows.

SPARE A COPPER
The male and female large copper butterflies, shown *left,* are now extinct in Great Britain but still to be found elsewhere in Europe and in Asia.

What is more, even if they do mature, they have a very short lifespan and may only live for four months at the most.

Caterpillars of the male and female Queen Alexandra's birdwing are identical – reddish-black with red pointed tentacles and a central cream area called a "saddle;" but the male and female butterflies are completely different. The males have blue and black wings, and their bright yellow bodies indicate they are poisonous. The females, meanwhile, are mainly brown and beige.

The government of Papua New Guinea has set up a program to protect the Queen Alexandra's birdwing butterfly. But attempts at conservation have not proved ideal.

Financial aid has also helped establish a number of butterfly farms which continue to "feed" the demand for specimens among collectors.

BRED IN CAPTIVITY

London's Natural History Museum, meanwhile, has welcomed the offer of a specimen of an entirely new species of butterfly, named after the man who accidentally bred it, naturalist Mark Lightowler. Different species of butterfly rarely interbreed, but he left together two live butterfly specimens – a Giant Owl from Honduras and a Splendid Owl from Costa Rica. As a result, five of an entirely new species – *Caligo Lightowlerii* (KAL-EE-GOH LEYE-TOWL-ER-EE-EE) – then metamorphosed.

These highly patterned brown and cream butterflies were not like either parent, only lived for a few days, but are expected to fetch more than $1,500 each.

One of the best ways to contribute to the preservation of butterflies is to create havens for them in the garden. It will encourage them to visit if you grow scented plants and wild flowers that are rich in nectar. Use of garden chemicals must also be avoided. On a global level too we need to give support to those who are working hard to save the world's endangered butterflies by maintaining the natural habitats of these most beautiful insects.

THE ST. HELENA EARWIG

The small South Atlantic island of St. Helena – to where Napoleon was exiled in 1815 and where he later died – is home to some very large species of insects. But not since the late 1960s has anyone seen the St.Helena giant earwig, now thought by some to be extinct.

The Danish entomologist Fabricius first described and named this amazing creepy-crawly in 1798. But the giant insect then became ignored until the mid-20th century.

According to an old wives' tale, earwigs were so-called because it was once thought they liked to crawl inside human ears if given half a chance. But even if this was true, you would not have needed to worry about an adult St. Helena earwig. It grew to be plump and to a length of 3 inches – a massive size for an earwig – and so could not possibly have got inside an ear.

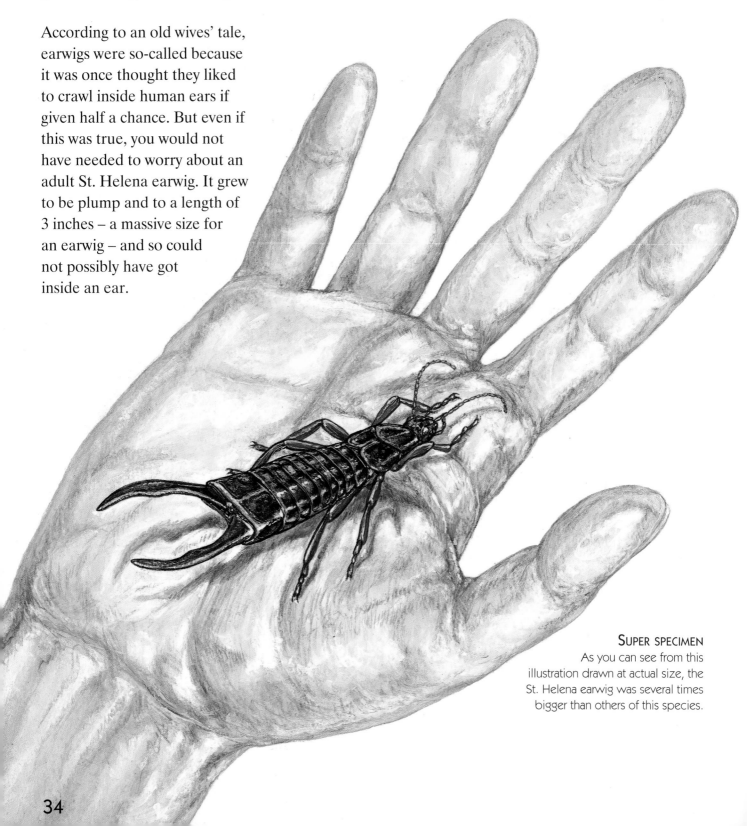

SUPER SPECIMEN
As you can see from this illustration drawn at actual size, the St. Helena earwig was several times bigger than others of this species.

Two ornithologists, who were studying bird life on St. Helena, happened to find the dead remains of a very large earwig and showed it to zoologists who mistook it for an entirely new species, naming it *Labidura loveridgei* (LAB-ID-OOR-AH LUV-ER-IJ-EE), after the scientist, Arthur Loveridge, to whom the specimen had first been given.

As the remains, which included the insect's pincers, were not fossilized, this suggested others of this species might still be alive on the island; and so in 1965 an expedition set off for St. Helena in search of the earwig. Several specimens were finally found; and as a result of careful study, it was realized the giant earwig was the very same species that Fabricus had described 170 years earlier. It is now known by the scientific name *Labidura herculeana* (LAB-EE-DOOR-AH HERK-YOO-LAHN-AH).

A further expedition was sent in 1988, but no more examples were unearthed, and none has been seen since. However, because this insect lives mostly underground, it may have eluded rediscovery. Other insect species exclusive to the island of St. Helena and thought to be extinct include the giant ground beetle and the St. Helena dragonfly.

LITTLE BROTHER
This photograph shows a common earwig on a daisy. It gives a clear indication of how enormous in comparison the elusive St. Helena earwig, shown *opposite*, was.

Recently, however, it was announced that the unique gumwood forests of St. Helena, which once covered one-third of the 27-square-mile island, were to be saved from extinction through a major conservation scheme designed to save other rare plant and animal life on the island too. The site, where thousands of these trees are being planted, is the very place where a St. Helena giant earwig was last seen before the area was

Fact file

- The last sightings of live St. Helena earwigs were made back in1965.

- In 1988 Great Britain's London Zoo sent a two-man team to the island of St. Helena to search for any surviving specimens of the giant earwig, but none was found. The expedition was known as *Project Hercules*, after the official scientific name (that of a hero in Greek mythology) given to this species of earwig.

- Most active at night, another reason why they are so elusive, earwigs have wings but tend only to take to the air on very hot days.

- The giant St. Helena earwig is reported to have had enormous pincers, used for capturing its insect prey.

abandoned and left to become a huge refuse dump. Many entomologists are hoping the assumption that this magnificent insect is now extinct will be proved wrong.

UNDERGROUND EXISTENCE
The image, *right*, shows the island of St. Helena to where the Emperor Napoleon was exiled in the 19th century and where the elusive giant earwig may still be living underground.

FAMOUS FINDS

Sometimes, creatures or plants are thought to be extinct but then suddenly reappear out of the blue. This, for example, was exactly what happened with the world's largest known species of beetle, the South American longhorn.

It may be hard to believe but there are more varieties of beetle than any other creature. In fact, one in every four animals known to exist is a member of the beetle family! Strangely too, the biggest beetle is also one of the rarest and most mysterious.

Titanus giganteus (<u>TIE</u>-TAN-US GEYE-<u>GANT</u>-EE-US), more commonly known as the South American longhorn beetle, is a shiny black insect that can grow up to eight inches in length. It was first named in 1778 by the famous Swedish scientist Carl Linnaeus, although he only ever saw an illustration of one.

For very many years, collectors searched in vain for a specimen in the Amazonian region of South America, where this beetle was known to live, but only dead longhorns came to light – until the early 20th century, that is.

FOUND IN A FISH

Back in 1910, as a native Brazilian Indian was going about his daily business of filleting fish caught in the river, he sliced one open and was astonished to discover a large, dead beetle nestling in its belly. He was about to throw it away when a German explorer, who happened to be nearby and therefore witnessed the chance find, asked if he could have a closer look at the giant bug.

SEASONAL SIGHTINGS
Huge but hard to find, the South American longhorn beetle, *left*, has proved easier to spot during the rainy season when it flies about.

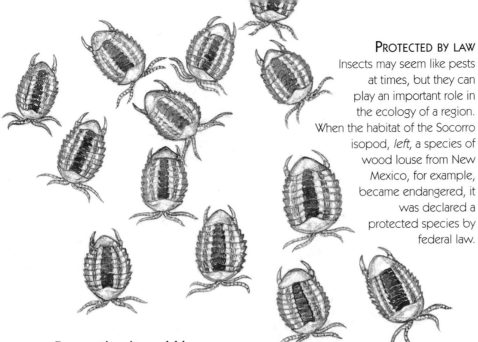

PROTECTED BY LAW
Insects may seem like pests at times, but they can play an important role in the ecology of a region. When the habitat of the Socorro isopod, *left*, a species of wood louse from New Mexico, for example, became endangered, it was declared a protected species by federal law.

Fact file

- One of the world's rarest flies – a two-inch-long insect with enormous wings – was captured by a five-year-old boy in 1987 in New Zealand. It had not previously been seen since 1941.

- As recently as 1992, an entomologist pointed out there is a species of Madagascan orchid that can only be pollinated by a moth with a 15-inch proboscis.

- In 1985 biologists in New Zealand discovered tiny creatures on a piece of driftwood and named them sea daisies, although they are not flowers, because of their petallike spines.

- The classification of organisms, both extinct and living, is known as taxonomy.

Suspecting it could be a *Titanus giganteus,* the explorer arranged for the specimen to be sent on to a team of entomologists who confirmed the identity of this rare beetle and who then offered to pay other Brazilian Indians to find more of these insects, since they could be sold to collectors for a substantial profit.

Live giant longhorn specimens remained scarce, however, until 1957 when "wanted" posters for the beetle, put up in a Brazilian mining camp, resulted in a number of finds.

DARWIN'S PREDICTION

The longhorn beetle had been known to exist, although hardly ever seen. Sometimes, though, scientists have been able to predict the existence of creatures never previously recorded. Charles Darwin, the great English naturalist, did just that. In 1862, as he examined an orchid from the island of Madagascar, off the east coast of Africa, Darwin noticed something strange.

For any insect to get at the nectar inside the flower, it would need a proboscis at least ten inches long. Such a creature was unknown on Madagascar, but Darwin was convinced one must exist because, clearly, not only was nectar being collected, the plant was being pollinated too.

Not everyone agreed with Darwin, but another expert went so far as to suggest that any such insect might be a larger relative of the African hawk moth, which has an 8-inch proboscis.

It was not until many years later, however, in 1903 that this new giant moth was found; and just as Darwin had predicted, it did indeed have a very long proboscis, extending to 11 inches – ideal for gathering nectar from the deepest of orchids.

FLOWERING ONCE MORE
The adder's tongue, a buttercup only growing in Gloucestershire, Great Britain, was formerly one of the world's rarest plants. Once endangered, it has been preserved and now produces many flowers.

LOST AND FOUND

Easter Island, the most remote inhabited island in the world, is renowned for its ancient statues and also the barren landscape. Yet acacialike trees once flourished there. Might they thrive again?

Easter Island (or *Rapa Nui* in its native Polynesian language) is a bleak, volcanic island in the Pacific Ocean, which lies some 2,200 miles west of the coast of Chile.

A JOURNAL ENTRY
Captain Cook recorded seeing the *Sophora toromiro* tree when he stopped at Easter Island in 1772.

MISSING TREES
Easter Island is home to nearly 900 giant statues, carved long ago when the island was covered in forests. The statues remain, but the trees have virtually all disappeared.

The island is world famous for the incredible statues of giant heads that were carved out of stone, mostly between 1400 and 1600. There are hundreds of these statues on the island, the largest 72 feet tall and weighing 160 tons.

Before the island became inhabited by people, visitors reported it was covered in forests of many different trees; and to plant-lovers, the island is most famous for a tree called *Sophora toromiro* (<u>SOF</u>-OR <u>AH</u> TO-ROH-<u>MEE</u>-RO) which resembles an acacia and grows to a height of just eight or nine feet.

FALLING NUMBERS

The *Sophora toromiro* was recorded in the journals of Captain Cook, who stopped at Easter Island when he sailed around the world in 1772.

Even then, the numbers of *Sophora toromiro* trees were dwindling as its wood was frequently used by the local population.

But when humans introduced goats, sheep, and cattle to the island in the 1860s, the tree's days were really numbered, and the last remaining specimens gradually died out as the animals stripped its bark.

It is thought the last *Sophora toromiro* tree on Easter Island was chopped down in 1962 to be used for firewood, and by the late 1970s, experts considered the tree to be extinct.

ALIVE AND WELL

It was then discovered, however, that the explorer Thor Heyerdahl visiting Easter Island in 1955 and 1956, had taken a seed pod from the last remaining tree located in a remote volcanic crater, although it was nearly dead at the time. Heyerdahl had then sent the seeds to a Swedish professor, who took them to a botanical garden in the city of Gothenburg, where two *Sophora toromiro* trees were already growing.

It was decided to try reintroducing the tree to Easter Island; but sadly, two attempts ended in failure. In 1994, however, a number of European botanical gardens set up a scheme specifically to preserve the *toromiro*.

HELPING HANDS

Some of the trees have now been planted on Easter Island, all originating from the seed pod gathered by Heyerdahl. With proper care and attention, it should be possible for the species to flourish once again in its native surroundings.

Fact file

- Thor Heyerdahl, an explorer and archaeologist from Norway, discovered Easter Island was once partially covered by wooded areas, but over many years the landscape was gradually deforested by its inhabitants.

- Thor Heyerdahl's research also showed Easter Island had been occupied from about 380AD, about one thousand years earlier than had been previously thought.

- Easter Island was once home to forests of palm trees, but these all died out as long ago as 1500.

- *Sophoro toromiro* is now grown in botanical gardens in Europe, Australia, and South America, as well as in some private gardens in Chile.

LEAVES OF PROMISE
The *Sophora toromiro* is a small tree with tiny, pale green leaves covered with delicate white strands of hair. Its seeds are yellow and are about the size of a pea. Once declared extinct, it now has a chance to grow again.

EXTINCT NO MORE

Not everything is doom and gloom in the world of conservation. Indeed, across these two pages you will find further fascinating examples of invertebrates and plants thought to have reached the brink of extinction but that suddenly turned up again.

One of the most surprising rediscoveries came in 1952 when marine biologists working on a research ship off the western coast of Mexico collected some specimens from 12,000 feet below the ocean.

Among them were a few examples of what looked like a small mollusk. On closer examination, however, scientists found it was not a present-day mollusk at all.

Instead, it was what is known as a "living fossil." Indeed, this invertebrate was thought to have died out 350 million years ago. To mark the fact that, in all that time, it had barely changed, the creature was given a new name – *Neopilina galatheae* (NEE-OH-PI-LEEN-AH GAH-LAH-THEE-EYE), meaning a new species of the *Pilina*, previously known only from fossils.

Galathea, meanwhile, was added after the ship that had retrieved the living fossil from the deep.

Neopilina was thin, just over an inch long, and almost transparent; but there was one other detail that fascinated scientists. Its body was like a worm's and divided into segments. Some experts therefore speculated at the time as to whether *Neopilina* may have been some sort of ancient link between mollusks and worms. Further research has shown, however, that mollusks and worms evolved entirely separately.

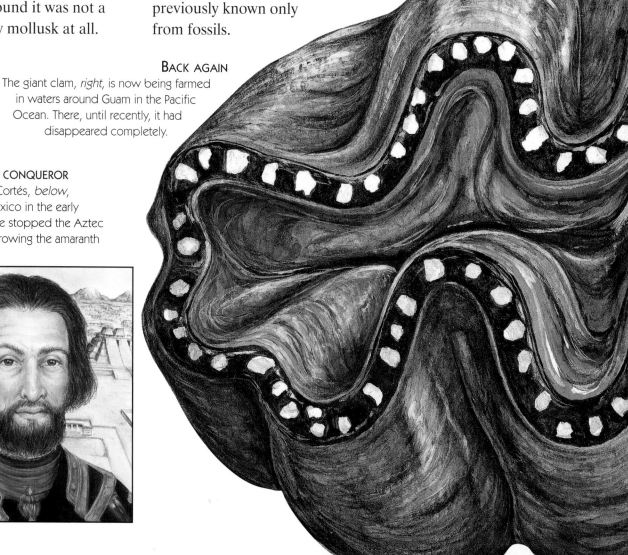

BACK AGAIN
The giant clam, *right*, is now being farmed in waters around Guam in the Pacific Ocean. There, until recently, it had disappeared completely.

BANNED BY A CONQUEROR
When Hernán Cortés, *below*, conquered Mexico in the early 16th century, he stopped the Aztec people from growing the amaranth plant, *far right*.

INSIDE STORY

Another intriguing creature from the sea is the white-toothed cowry. The first specimen to be identified was found by chance in a collection of shells bought by the British Museum in the mid 19th century. Subsequently, *Cypraea leucodon* (KIP-REYE-AH LOOK-OH-DON) was classed as one of the world's rarest seashells. In 1963, however, a conchologist (the name given to an enthusiast who studies shells) was presented with a photograph of one found in the belly of a fish.

More recently, examples have also been found in the Philippines and Maldives. Collectors prize this beautiful shell highly, and it is even possible to buy specimens through sites on the Internet.

FIND THE KING!

You might think the world's largest bee could not stay hidden for long, but it was as recently as 1859 that the so-called king bee was first described. Found on a small Indonesian island and black except for pale cheeks and a reddish face, it is nearly two inches long, with huge mouthparts. Since then, it has remained hard to find because it does not build a nest but lives with termites.

Fact file

● A primitive ant from Australia with very large eyes, thought to have gone extinct by the 1940s, was rediscovered in 1977. It has the scientific name *Nothomyrmecia macrops* (NOH-THOH-MYR-MEES-EE-AH MAK-ROPS).

● *Trichoplax* (TREYEK-OH-PLAX) was first discovered in an aquarium in Austria in 1883. Flat and like an amoeba, although multi-cellular, it can only be seen under the microscope and was rediscovered in 1971.

● An ancestor of modern crabs, lobsters, and other crustaceans, the *Neoglyphea* (NEE-OH-GLIF-EE-AH) was thought to have become extinct 50 million years ago, but made a reappearance during the 20th century near the islands of the Philippines.

DYEING OUT

The amaranth or love-lies-bleeding plant of Mexico, *below*, almost became extinct. Once used by the ancient Aztecs to make a red dye for their ceremonies, the Spanish conquerer Cortés stopped it being grown as part of his persecution of their religion. Now, however, it is being reintroduced and is highly prized.

PRESERVING INSECT LIFE

Some insects can be a terrible nuisance. They bite us, chew away at clothes, damage wood, contaminate food, carry disease, or destroy crops. Why, then, should we listen to entomologists when they point out how vital it is to protect most of them?

Bees, wasps, and beetles are just three examples of those insects we should certainly respect.

Without them, we would be unlikely ever to enjoy another chocolate bar, bananas, beans, or a whole variety of other foods. Our gardens would probably be devoid of color, too. Quite simply, these insects are prime pollinators and vital to the survival of most of the world's vegetation. In the search for nectar, they accidentally gather pollen on their bodies and carry it from male parts of the flowers to the female parts.

Seeds can then be produced for a new generation of that particular plant.

Perhaps surprisingly, ants, moths, and butterflies are also responsible for pollinating angiosperms (flowering plants.) Indeed, the interaction between all such insects and the plants they help to reproduce is a constant source of wonder.

The males of one species of butterfly, for instance, visit specific flowers to collect a certain chemical that will attract the females to them. The females then use this substance to coat their eggs, and this in turn protects the eggs from risk of attack by ants.

Although the wind sometimes contributes to successful pollination, many thousands of plants are entirely reliant upon insect pollinators for survival. We humans, meanwhile – described by one angry entomologist as an exterminator species – are only just waking up to the fact that, in the past, we have often been neglectful of the insects' needs, as we wilfully killed them or destroyed their natural habitats, so that plants failed to flourish.

LADY POWER

Scientists estimate that on average every year, almost half of all crops are destroyed by some sort of insect pest. Use of pesticides can help to prevent this, but even those targeted to kill specific species may also kill helpful insects. The smallholder or vegetable gardener who is concerned about the environment therefore often encourages ladybugs to his plot. Colorado beetle larvae will not stand a chance against this small but greedy brigade, and so potato plants should not suffer too much damage.

SPRAYING AWAY
When helicopters spray insecticides to rid agricultural land of insect pests, as in the photograph *above*, there is always the risk other creatures may become contaminated.

Fact file

● Insects are known to make excellent bio-indicators. Indeed, entomologists are sometimes called on to monitor insect populations in specific areas for signs of local environmental damage.

● Hundreds of different species of insects are eaten regularly worldwide. It is vital, however, not to try them without first checking they are definitely not poisonous. Some can be lethal.

● Some earth-dwelling insects, such as ants, help to keep the soil in good condition.

● Wasps will pollinate flowers but also make themselves useful in the garden by feeding not only themselves but their young on the larvae of some of the worst garden pests.

Indeed, entire ecosystems will be in danger of collapse if some species of insects become severely endangered and head toward extinction.

GOOD HEALTH!

But there is another very important reason to preserve certain insects. Increasingly, researchers are finding some release substances that can be helpful in combating disease and dangerous medical conditions affecting both animals and human beings.

In the past, before the widespread use of antibiotics, for instance, maggots would be placed on wounds to speed the healing of infected wounds. Veterinary surgeons sometimes use a secretion of the Spanishfly beetle to ease skin conditions in animals.

Meanwhile, in humans, bee venom has been shown to increase blood flow and relieve rheumatism; and research seems to indicate that a substance found in butterfly wings could possibly be of use in treating some forms of cancer. Traditional Chinese medicine also involves the use of many insect compounds.

Entomologists point out too that by preserving certain insects we may be able to provide an inexpensive source of valuable protein for those in

countries where famine has struck. Not all insects are edible but stir-fried ants and steamed cicadas are even regarded as delicacies in some parts of the world.

SAVE OUR HEDGEROWS!
Hedgerows, like the one shown here, provide such an ideal habitat for beneficial insects and pest-predators that in some parts of the world there are now regulations to protect them.

Saving the World's Flora

The Millennium Seed Bank (so called because it was launched in the year 2000) is based at a branch of Great Britain's internationally renowned Kew Gardens. At this center botanists are busy creating what has been described as a Noah's Ark for plant life.

Frozen assets
Most seeds held by the bank at Kew Gardens, *above*, are frozen so that they should be viable for 200 years.

With every passing year, all over the world, as natural habitats are increasingly destroyed through human action, more and more plant life is becoming severely depleted. Some types of vegetation, having evolved over millions of years, even seem to have disappeared altogether; and the situation for a number of rare plants is now dire.

How wonderful it would be if we could suddenly call a halt to environmental destruction and thereby save all the world's plant life! For the moment, though, that is highly unlikely on anything approaching a global scale. Something therefore has to be done to ensure future generations can benefit from our planet's flora to the full. That is why scientists are now busy drying, bottling, and freezing countless types of seed as a sort of insurance policy, just in case these plants become further endangered in their natural habitats for whatever reason.

Seeds, it seems, have an extraordinarily long shelf-life. Some that were hundreds of years old have been known to germinate even though not frozen, so prospects should be good for those stored at a very low temperature. The aim is to have 20% of all known plants in the newly established seed bank by the year 2020.

A brilliant scheme
Botanists from many other countries are cooperating with the scientists working at Kew by providing samples of seeds from the world's most arid regions in case these plants ever become extinct in the wild. Seeds from such dry environments can generally be left dormant and stored for long periods, as shown *left*, without any effect on germination.

A HEALTHY START
The photograph, *left,* shows frozen seeds starting to germinate in a small dish in the laboratory, much to the delight of the scientist involved in the experiment.

This very worthwhile effort will cost over $100 million. This may sound an enormous amount of money but the scheme, which scientists believe is a very practical conservation option since it is not always possible to protect plants in their natural environment, is partly sponsored by industry. It is also likely to be cost-effective in the long run because of the tremendous benefits it will bring. Twenty-five percent of all the medicines currently prescribed are plant-derived, for example; and it could well be that many more such naturally occurring cures will be found in years to come.

The plan is that all seeds will be stored in glass jars at a temperature of -20 degrees Celsius; and in each of these jars, because seeds take up such little space, scientists working at the bank hope it may be possible to place many hundreds of thousands of seeds for each species to be preserved in this way.

Scientists are also optimistic that 80% of the seeds gathered for this scheme can safely be stored at such a low temperature for 200 years at least, while some should survive far longer, perhaps even for thousands of years, so that scientists alive today will never themselves know whether they remained viable – unless, that is, our lifespan can be significantly extended through storage at a very low temperature prior to death and decay. It is not beyond the realms of possibility and has been an area of research for some years.

No one knows whether or not this science, known as *cryogenics* (<u>KREYE</u>-OH-<u>JEN</u>-IKS), will ever be further developed so that, at the touch of a button, humans of today may at any specified time be reawoken from a long sleep. But, at least in theory, as a result of the establishment of Great Britain's Millennium Seed Bank, botanists of the future should be able to replenish the world with any plants that by that point in time have become endangered or extinct in their natural habitat.

STORED AT LOW TEMPERATURES
The scientist in this photograph wears a mask and protective clothing as he works with a freezing process to preserve rare seeds.

Fact file

- Seed hunters are now working all the way around the world to collect samples for the Millennium Seed Bank that is based in Great Britain. Many other countries – among them the United States, Lebanon, Australia, and South Africa – are cooperating with the scheme.

- Botanists claim that many of the world's wild plants are more threatened today than at any time since the last Ice Age.

- Proof that seeds can indeed survive cold storage came when, after 25 years at a very low temperature, a cock's-foot plant, known scientifically as *Dactylis* (<u>DAKT</u>-EEL-IS) sprouted at the first attempt.

- Humans are dependent on plants for food, raw materials, and some medicines.

It may be the only way we can attempt to save our planet's wonderful natural heritage for eternity.

GLOSSARY

algae
tiny, stemless plants occurring in water or on moist ground

amoeba
a tiny, primitive organism that continually changes shape

antibiotics
medicines to fight infections

bacteria
microscopic causes of many diseases

botanist
someone who studies plant life

camouflage
disguise to avoid being seen

carnivore
a meat-eater

conservation
preservation of the environment

Cretaceous times
a period lasting from about 144 to 65 million years ago

deforestation
the removal of forests

DNA
deoxyribonucleic (DEE-OX-EE-REYE-BOH NOO-KLAY-IK) acid, a substance passing on hereditary characteristics

ecology
study of the environment

ecosystem
interaction of living organisms

entomologist
someone who studies insect life

flora
plants and other vegetation

gargantuan
enormous

gastropods
a group of creatures comprising snails, slugs, whelks, and others

germinate
to begin to grow

graft
to take a piece of one plant to form new plant growth

habitat
the natural environment of an animal or plant

herbivore
a plant-eater

insecticide
a substance killing insects

insectivore
an insect-eater

Jurassic times
a period lasting from about 213 to 144 million years ago

lichens (LEYE-KENS)
small plants formed by fungi and algae on bark or ground

Mesozoic times
an era covering Triassic, Jurassic, and Cretaceous times

metamorphose
to change from one form to another

ovules
female parts of plants that, after fertilization, become seeds

paleobotanist
a scientist who studies prehistoric plant life

paleontologist
a scientist who studies fossils

Paleozoic
a long era lasting from about 570 to 230 million years ago

petrified
fossilized or turned to stone

proboscis
an insect's elongated mouthparts

rhizome
a type of underground root

smog
fog due to pollution

symbiotic
relying on each other

FAMOUS FINDS

Sometimes, creatures or plants are thought to be extinct but then suddenly reappear out of the blue. This, for example, was exactly what happened with the world's largest known species of beetle, the South American longhorn.

It may be hard to believe but there are more varieties of beetle than any other creature. In fact, one in every four animals known to exist is a member of the beetle family! Strangely too, the biggest beetle is also one of the rarest and most mysterious.

Titanus giganteus (TIE-TAN-US GEYE-GANT-EE-US), more commonly known as the South American longhorn beetle, is a shiny black insect that can grow up to eight inches in length. It was first named in 1778 by the famous Swedish scientist Carl Linnaeus, although he only ever saw an illustration of one.

For very many years, collectors searched in vain for a specimen in the Amazonian region of South America, where this beetle was known to live, but only dead longhorns came to light – until the early 20th century, that is.

FOUND IN A FISH

Back in 1910, as a native Brazilian Indian was going about his daily business of filleting fish caught in the river, he sliced one open and was astonished to discover a large, dead beetle nestling in its belly. He was about to throw it away when a German explorer, who happened to be nearby and therefore witnessed the chance find, asked if he could have a closer look at the giant bug.

SEASONAL SIGHTINGS
Huge but hard to find, the South American longhorn beetle, *left*, has proved easier to spot during the rainy season when it flies about.

Two ornithologists, who were studying bird life on St. Helena, happened to find the dead remains of a very large earwig and showed it to zoologists who mistook it for an entirely new species, naming it *Labidura loveridgei* (<u>LAB</u>-ID-<u>OOR</u>-AH <u>LUV</u>-ER-IJ-EE), after the scientist, Arthur Loveridge, to whom the specimen had first been given.

As the remains, which included the insect's pincers, were not fossilized, this suggested others of this species might still be alive on the island; and so in 1965 an expedition set off for St. Helena in search of the earwig. Several specimens were finally found; and as a result of careful study, it was realized the giant earwig was the very same species that Fabricus had described 170 years earlier. It is now known by the scientific name *Labidura herculeana* (<u>LAB</u>-EE-<u>DOOR</u>-AH <u>HERK</u>-YOO-<u>LAHN</u>-AH).

A further expedition was sent in 1988, but no more examples were unearthed, and none has been seen since. However, because this insect lives mostly underground, it may have eluded rediscovery. Other insect species exclusive to the island of St. Helena and thought to be extinct include the giant ground beetle and the St. Helena dragonfly.

LITTLE BROTHER
This photograph shows a common earwig on a daisy. It gives a clear indication of how enormous in comparison the elusive St. Helena earwig, shown *opposite*, was.

Recently, however, it was announced that the unique gumwood forests of St. Helena, which once covered one-third of the 27-square-mile island, were to be saved from extinction through a major conservation scheme designed to save other rare plant and animal life on the island too. The site, where thousands of these trees are being planted, is the very place where a St. Helena giant earwig was last seen before the area was

Fact file

● The last sightings of live St. Helena earwigs were made back in 1965.

● In 1988 Great Britain's London Zoo sent a two-man team to the island of St. Helena to search for any surviving specimens of the giant earwig, but none was found. The expedition was known as *Project Hercules*, after the official scientific name (that of a hero in Greek mythology) given to this species of earwig.

● Most active at night, another reason why they are so elusive, earwigs have wings but tend only to take to the air on very hot days.

● The giant St. Helena earwig is reported to have had enormous pincers, used for capturing its insect prey.

abandoned and left to become a huge refuse dump. Many entomologists are hoping the assumption that this magnificent insect is now extinct will be proved wrong.

UNDERGROUND EXISTENCE
The image, *right*, shows the island of St. Helena to where the Emperor Napoleon was exiled in the 19th century and where the elusive giant earwig may still be living underground.